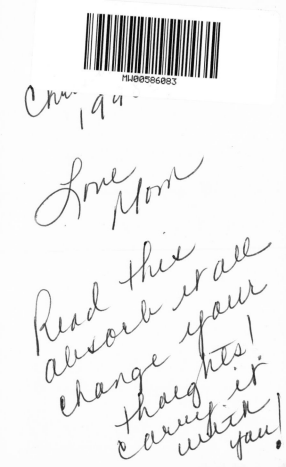

Chr~~~ 19~~

Love
Mom

Read this
absorb it all
change your
thoughts!
carry it
with
you!

THE
MENTAL GAME
POCKET
COMPANION
FOR GOLF

FRAN PIROZZOLO with RUSS PATE

HarperPerennial
A Division of HarperCollinsPublishers

HarperCollins books may be purchased for educational, business, or sales promotional use. For information, please write: Special Markets Department, HarperCollins Publishers, Inc., 10 East 53rd Street, New York, NY 10022.

FIRST EDITION

Library of Congress Cataloging-in-Publication Data
Pirozzolo, Francis J.
    The mental game pocket companion for golf / Fran Pirozzolo with Russ Pate. — 1st ed.
        p.   cm.
    ISBN 0-06-273397-4
    1. Golf—Psychological aspects. I. Pate, Russ. II. Title.
GV979.P75P57   1966
796.352'01'9—dc20   96-10656

96 97 98 99 00 ❖/RRD 10 9 8 7 6 5 4 3 2 1

INTRODUCTION

The goal of *The Mental Game Pocket Companion* is to help readers become better golfers. It is my belief that golf—perhaps as much as any other sport—is fundamentally a game in which the "battle within yourself" is paramount. Golf represents a battle to make the swings you know how to make; to keep your mind focused on the shot you're trying to hit; to keep yourself positive; and to control your thoughts and emotions.

In this book you will find the "secrets" of success in golf. These secrets are the methods and strategies of mental training shared by many truly great athletes. While I wish I could say I discovered these secrets, the fact is they've been around for thousands of years and can be found in the psychology and philosophy of such great thinkers as Socrates, Epictetus, Seneca, Sun Tsu and many others.

This pocket companion is organized into a series of instructional lessons, or tips, which will enable you to learn from golf legends like Ben Hogan, Byron Nelson and Sam Snead. You will also learn the secrets of how modern stars like Greg Norman, Fred Couples and Bernhard Langer manage themselves on the course.

These tips have been inspired by great leaders, coaches and thinkers of our time and others who have given us many of the answers about the importance of self-regulation, faith in oneself, playing under pressure and developing a winner's attitude.

What follows is a synthesis of the great lessons I have been exposed to—as an athlete, student, fan, coach and sports psychologist. I am fortunate that the associations I've had enable me to summarize the concepts presented in this book. I have had the greatest teachers possible—the athletes themselves—

who have shared their experiences with me. I have been able to witness their performances either from the closeness of an intimate friendship or the protected environment of a clinical relationship.

I have caddied in major golf championships, been at ringside in heavyweight championship bouts, sat in a major league baseball dugout, watched in awe as the space shuttle carried friends into orbit around the earth and taken my own lumps in football, baseball, wrestling and golf.

With the perspective I've gained, it's clear to me that winning the battle within yourself is the most difficult challenge. What stops us from thinking more clearly? Why can't we be honest with ourselves about what we can and cannot do? Why do we engage in such self-disparagement and self-abuse? Why do we allow fear, anxiety and bad attitudes to control our thinking?

Confidence is a word used widely in every sport. But what is confidence, why does it seem to fluctuate and how can we get more of it? There is no question the most powerful force in sports is the mood of the moment—the feeling that you can accomplish whatever you need to do.

Confidence means "with faith." And faith, like confidence, is something you can't fake. It is the result of talent, the right attitude, hard work and persistence.

How do readers develop more confidence in themselves and their golf games? The formula is found in this book:

- You assess your skills (mental and physical) and determine how to develop each skill to the highest possible level;
- You get rid of bad attitudes and belief systems that simply don't work;
- You set good goals for your practices and competitions;

- You prepare yourself in the best possible way—mentally and physically;
- You discipline yourself to focus on what you need to do to get the most out of yourself;
- You learn to make the most out of your good shots and your mistakes; and
- You learn how to think constructively and to talk to yourself in ways that encourage better performance, more fun and peaking—not folding up under pressure.

The first section of this book introduces readers to some of the over-arching principles of a better mental game. It reveals how to train our minds for competition and how to attune ourselves for our best golf. The exercises and drills presented in the final section of the book will enable you to improve quickly and to adopt the right attitudes.

The purpose of this book is twofold: to explain how golfers can minimize the pressure, tension, fear and negative emotions they experience on the golf course; and to explain how golfers can develop the mental toughness they need to play their best golf. I have assembled a team of experts to prescribe the proper countermeasures for dealing with self-consciousness, self-criticism and self-doubt—obstacles that impair performance and dilute the pleasure players derive from the game.

The good news for readers is that these obstacles can be confronted and overcome. By understanding yourself better and learning how to apply proper countermeasures when those tough moments arise, as they invariably will, you can free yourself from the shackles of self-limiting thinking and defeatism.

The good news is that the battle within yourself can be won.

—Francis J. Pirozzolo, Ph.D.

TIP #1:
GUIDING LIGHT

Marcus Aurelius once observed that a person's life is what his or her thoughts make it.

Use that centuries-old piece of wisdom as a guiding light for your own development in golf. If your thoughts on the golf course are positive and focused, you will increase your performance state. If your thoughts are negative and cluttered, you will diminish your performance state.

Assuming you reach some degree of physical competency in golf, your thoughts—as Aurelius might have put it—will ultimately determine what kind of golfer you will become.

Perhaps the greatest hockey player of all time,
Mario Lemieux is successful because of the
superior quality of his mental skills.

TIP #2:
DON'T BE A COPYCAT

Amateur golfers, in the endless (though usually misguided) quest for improvement, often seek to copy the swings of the most accomplished players in the game. Although that premise seems reasonable, the great Bobby Jones criticized golfers who tried to learn the game by emulating "expert models." Jones warned that "trying studiously to imitate the method of another" was one of the most serious handicaps for amateur golfers. A better strategy for developing your own skills in golf is to invest in the physical practice required, then absorb the systematic feedback from performance and results (trial and error). If you want to emulate anything about a premier player like Greg Norman, copy his high-performance attitude, his belief in himself, his commitment to training and—perhaps most of all—his absolute refusal to surrender to bad breaks and tough luck.

Hal Sutton endured a long slump that was caused by changing his swing—in spite of the fact that he hit the ball as well as anyone in the world.

TIP #3:
LEARNING GOLF

Many golfers go through life without learning how to play the game. They spend 100 percent of the time thinking (or worrying) about the motor skills and mechanics required to swing a club—the so-called "science" of golf—while ignoring the art of playing golf, the attentional and affective sets of skills that golf requires.

A generation of American golfers grew up seeking to copy Jack Nicklaus' upright swing. But how many of those golfers took to heart one of Nicklaus' most revealing insights: "I have never hit a shot, not even in practice, without having a very sharp, in-focus picture of it in my head."

And even Ben Hogan, golf's ultimate grinder, attributed his success to an attitude change. Hogan stopped trying to develop a "perfect" golf swing because, as he put it, "It became clear in my mind that this ambitious over-thoroughness was neither advisable nor even necessary."

Imagine, Ben Hogan, golf's perfectionist, imploring fellow golfers not to go overboard in their pursuit of physical prowess.

We recommend redirecting a percentage of the time and energy you devote to your golf swing to learning what constitutes a strong mental game.

TIP #4:
FACING FEAR

The noted Greek philosopher Aristotle recognized that how we face "dangerous situations"—either with confidence or fear—makes us brave or cowardly.

How we *act* when challenged reveals our character and nature. If we are always angry or out-of-control, then this will be our habit when faced with adversity.

All great golfers have fears, but they learn to overcome them by recognizing the fear and confronting it. They employ such countermeasures as self-trust, positive self-talk, relaxation and keeping a good perspective.

Aristotle taught that how we act under pressure reveals our character.

TIP #5:
LEARNING MENTAL
TOUGHNESS

We've all heard the argument that "experience is the best teacher." But experiences come in many forms: through our mistakes, through the example of others and through explicit instruction. Whether you learn how to relax through biofeedback, through meditation or prayer or through learning to talk to yourself more positively doesn't matter at all. What does matter is that you learn the mechanism—and that you own it!

Similarly, mental toughness can be learned through your own battles with adversity or from your golf teacher, partner or priest. The point is that you learn it from someone.

Mental toughness is the ability to be absorbed in the task, to block out distraction, to be aggressive and positive and to respond to failure when it inevitably occurs. Working on mental toughness may mean having to change some beliefs that haven't been productive for you, but with commitment to improving yourself and your game, it can be done.

It's important to recognize that even great golfers have some beliefs and attitudes that are less than optimal. They need to let go of things that don't work for them. So do you.

TIP #6:
THE SADDEST STATISTIC
IN GOLF

Despite the hope held out by "hot" golf balls, revolutionary new shafts and ultra-forgiving clubheads, the sad truth is that only a small percentage of golfers ever improve. Handicap statistics compiled by the National Golf Foundation and United States Golf Association show that most golfers establish a level of competency after a few years and afterward seldom vary in ability by more than a stroke or two.

Why don't golfers improve more? And why don't more golfers improve? The answers probably can be traced to improper training. Golfers tend to get wrapped up in equipment issues and are consumed by the physical game. They tend to ignore the mental side of golf and mastering the short game.

Improvement in golf doesn't come from some "magic move" you can order from a telemarketer. Nor is it likely to be found in the latest new swing theory. After all, the fundamentals of the modern swing have been in place for more than a half-century, ever since people like Walter Hagen, Gene Sarazen and Bobby Jones emerged as America's first golf heroes.

Improvement in golf can only be achieved by building, through repetition, a reasonably consistent swing and then conquering the mental roadblocks of fear, anxiety and negative self-expression, which undermine performance.

TIP #7:
GEAR UP FOR THE
CHALLENGE

Successful golfers develop the proper on-course attitude, namely, the determination to respond to challenges they face. They take to heart the timeless advice that Jackie Burke Jr., the former Masters and PGA champion, gives his pupils:

"Be prepared to scramble, right from the first tee."

This gem from Burke's own playing philosophy correctly assumes that golfers will make mistakes and experience bad breaks. Burke knew that being mentally ready to face any challenge, and having the mental toughness to overcome adversity, are qualities that separate champions from the rest of the pack.

Al Del Greco and Fran Pirozzolo discuss how to conquer the challenges.

TIP #8:
AVOID GOLF'S DEATH MOVES

Bad golf isn't necessarily a function of poor swings or faulty decisions. Prime performance-wreckers, in many cases, are negative thoughts, images and attitudes. Some of the prevalent morbid attitudes in golf—the so-called "death moves"—are:

1. Over-generalization—"I made double-bogey on the first hole, so I'll probably make double-bogey on the next hole as well."
2. Awfulizing or Catastrophizing—"Missing that short putt on the last hole was the worst thing that's ever happened to me!"
3. Exaggerating Importance—"I work so hard at this game. It consumes my whole life. Why don't I play any better?"
4. Excessive Expectations—"I should be able to hit any shot when needed. Draws, fades, punch shots, chips, pitches, flop wedges, the works."
5. Irrational Denial—"People say that I'd play better if I would lighten up, but what do they know? I'll just get away from everyone, so I don't have to deal with this."

Golfers with mental toughness can talk themselves into having a good round. Golfers lacking mental toughness, almost assuredly, will talk themselves into having a bad round.

*Teaching pro Jim McLean coined the term
"death moves" for certain physical mistakes
and the term is equally applicable to the
mental game.*

TIP #9:
BRING OUT YOUR BEST COMPETITIVE SIDE

A good competitor in golf enjoys all challenges associated with a round—from playing the course to competing against others. He or she doesn't focus on negatives or whine about playing conditions or become distracted by water sprinklers, the grounds crew or slow play. A good competitor just keeps on keeping on. If you're a poor competitor, or a noncompetitor, you should decide which areas of your game need work. Are your deficiencies related to the full swing? The short game? How is your mental game? Course management?

You can set out to become more competitive by becoming more systematic in your acquisition of golf skills. Then, when you head to the golf course, take along the right attitudes. Love the challenge, exercise patience, have self-trust, and be relaxed, ready and eager to play.

By being performance-oriented—and not obsessed with the outcome—you will naturally bring out your best competitive instincts.

Maybe the best quarterback of all time, Dan Marino brings out the best in himself.

TIP #10:
BEING COMPETITIVE
WHILE HAVING FUN

Having fun playing golf implies staying in the present, going with the flow, enjoying the moment and not being concerned with the outcome, or results.

Some golfers erroneously think that golf, by its nature, must be a struggle. They do not believe that the concept of "fun" can apply to such a challenging, complicated task—especially when competition (like a friendly wager) is involved.

In truth, having fun and being competitive go hand-in-hand. If you're staying in the present moment and not worrying about ego, if you're not worried about your standing relative to par or other players, then you are headed toward your peak performance state.

As a by-product, you're having more fun.

Two great competitors, Charles Barkley and Danny Ainge, having fun.

TIP #11:
LOSING IS AN ATTITUDE

Just as winning is an attitude, so is losing. Losers—by which we mean self-defeatists—have developed patterns of thinking that are self-limiting.

Signs of a losing mentality are clear: Losers may get ahead in a match and then, inexplicably, choose high-risk strategies when better options exist; losers may respond to success by entertaining randomly chaotic thoughts, such as "now that I have improved to this level, I should change my swing"; losers may actually work harder at the game than winners, but their efforts are unfocused and counterproductive.

Losers, ironically, may know exactly how to help another athlete by providing timely advice ("relax, you're trying too hard"), but losers fail to heed their own advice. Losers fail to follow the examples set by winners: Have fun, enjoy the challenge and stretch yourself to the limits of your ability.

TIP #12:
NOT MINDING VERSUS
NOT CARING

"**N**ot caring" about your performance in golf is one thing. Not caring implies not being motivated, not having goals, not working hard to succeed.

"Not minding" about your performance is something altogether different. Not minding is a healthy mental approach to have.

Not minding implies being mentally tough. It means not worrying about the outcome of a particular shot or what others think about your swing. It means not conceding anything when conditions are difficult or your opponent is having a good day or the breaks aren't going your way.

Not minding is a powerful mental concept for a golfer to adopt. When taken to its fullest extent, it means you will not allow into your consciousness anything that is peripheral to helping you do your job.

TIP #13:
THINK LIKE A
CHAMPION

Here are five mental characteristics that separate golf champions from underachievers:

1. An exceptional degree of self-trust and self-acceptance.
2. An extraordinary independence from their environment and an unusual ability to remain detached from what is going on around them.
3. An efficient perception of reality and a comfortable relationship with it.
4. A problem-centered, goal-oriented and achievement-motivated attitude.
5. A capacity for vivid appreciation and a childlike quality of seeing something new or good in almost every experience.

Golf is not simply a test of physical skills; if it were, you could hold all the pro tournaments on the practice tee. Rather, golf is primarily a mental test. More often than not, the champion is the golfer that thinks the best, has the most positive thoughts, absorbs himself or herself in the experience, gets in the zone and goes with the flow.

Thinking like a champion is the key to success.

TIP #14:
SELF–TRUST

Self-trust and confidence fit together in the mental game of golf. They emanate from the answer to one fundamental question: "Do I possess the skills to get this task done?"

Augmenting self-trust is the critical dimension of positive self-talk. By that, we mean talking to yourself in a way that will enhance your motivation to succeed and not wear down your interest in the game.

Many golfers find that self-trust is eroded by self-limiting thoughts. These are thoughts based on past experiences ("I always hit in this bunker; I probably will again") or thoughts that are outcome-based and demeaning to your character and self.

Self-limiting thoughts are often irrational. They demonstrate a lack of self-awareness.

Has there ever been an athlete who, under pressure, trusts himself more than John Elway of the Denver Broncos?

TIP #15:
ATTITUDE IS (ALMOST) EVERYTHING

The lines of demarcation in the mental game of golf are clear. You don't need to be a sports psychologist to recognize that some attitudes are productive and promote good play, while other attitudes are counterproductive and prohibit good play.

Performance-enhancing attitudes include:
- Having self-trust
- Loving the challenge
- Having fun
- Playing in the present
- Being relaxed, ready and focused
- Being performance-oriented
- Having high intrinsic motivation

Performance-killing attitudes include:
- Fear
- Experiencing anxiety or tension
- Being self-conscious
- Trying too hard or not being committed
- Playing in the past or future
- Being results-oriented
- Having low intrinsic motivation

Understand the difference and work to develop the proper frame of mind, and you'll see dramatic improvement in your own play.

TIP #16:
SELF–ACCEPTANCE

Great golfers accept themselves and their golf games. They accept their shortcomings, realizing that because they are human beings, they will make mistakes.

That does not mean they are self-satisfied. They constantly strive to improve. But they are not crippled by the knowledge that their golf swings are imperfect.

Acceptance leads to trust, and trust leads to confidence. When a golfer accepts himself and trusts himself, he can be patient. He can suppress the tendency to want to force the issue, to see immediate effects from all his hard work.

You can't force the issue in golf. You can seize the moment of opportunity, but you can't, as the Chinese like to say, "push the river."

Self-acceptance brings you to terms with that realization.

TIP #17:
INDEPENDENCE FROM
THE ENVIRONMENT

Great golfers share the characteristic of detachment, the ability to stay within themselves and play their own game. They are not affected by bad weather, galleries, bad pairings or other potentially adverse conditions. They are relatively independent of the favorable opinion of others. They are relatively happy and serene in the midst of circumstances that may discourage lesser players.

Great golfers are mentally strong enough to be self-controlled. They don't worry about what other players think about their swings. The honors, awards, rewards and status they achieve from golf are less important to them than self-development, self-improvement and inner growth.

Two of the toughest basketball players ever, Charles Barkley and Danny Ainge learned long ago that you have to be detached from your surroundings to be your best. You can't succeed against a hostile crowd unless you remain detached and play your own game.

TIP #18:
AN EFFICIENT PERCEPTION
OF REALITY

All of us have little neuroses that affect how we perceive the world. We can prejudice our perception of reality by not being able to see ourselves, or our environment, as it really is.

Underachievers at golf often attempt heroic (read: foolish) shots on the course. Their perception doesn't jibe with reality.

Great golfers have a comfortable relationship with reality. They know what they can—and cannot—do. They know, for example, that they can't use a 6-iron for a 210-yard carry over water. They don't try to perform anything they have not previously rehearsed, either on the practice tee or the golf course.

TIP #19:
A PROBLEM–CENTERED,
GOAL–ORIENTED ATTITUDE

Great golfers establish long-term goals that are realistic and achievable. More importantly, they understand the work required to accomplish those goals.

All golfers would benefit from having a specific set of short-term goals for improvement. These goals, which should either be put in writing or shared with someone such as a friend or coach, will keep golfers focused on a specific target. They serve to remind us what we're working on and committed to.

TIP #20:
BEING IN THE ZONE

Professional athletes often refer to their periods of peak performance as "being in the zone." Golfers from the era of Byron Nelson, Ben Hogan and Sam Snead called this phenomenon "the trance."

The elements of being in the zone, or trance, are:
1. Concentrating on the immediate task.
2. Having clear goals.
3. Letting go of control (but, paradoxically, exercising control of yourself).
4. Losing yourself in the task (which triggers a feeling of unself-consciousness and a lack of worry about what the outcome might mean to you).
5. A transformation of the experience of time, especially the ability to make time slow down.

Unfortunately, golfers can't make the zone happen automatically. They can't force it or push it. In fact, the more a golfer tries to make it happen, the farther you get from it.

Allow yourself a better chance to enter the "zone."

TIP #21:
CONCENTRATION

Concentration is a key to better performance, and learning how to take control over your concentration will speed your development as a golfer.

A useful metaphor is that your mind is a camera, which registers images the lens focuses upon. You must train yourself to adjust the lens to bring into awareness what is really worth focusing upon.

The camera (mind) has a wide-angle lens and a narrow-angle lens. At times, the lens needs to be adjusted so we capture information from a broad area, like when studying a dogleg fairway from the tee. At other times, we need to focus narrowly or zoom in on a discrete target, like when reading a putt.

Concentration exercises have been around for generations. Baseball players from earlier eras, for example, developed concentration skills by staring at an object, without blinking, for long periods of time. Not surprisingly, players who could do this task best were generally great hitters—such as Ted Williams, the Boston Red Sox Hall of Famer who was said to have the longest blink-rate ever measured.

*A useful metaphor for the golfer's mind: It's
like a camera lens in its ability to focus.*

TIP #22:
VIVID APPRECIATION

Great golfers love playing golf. They enjoy the sheer physical act of swinging a club and hitting a ball. They revel in the challenge of executing shots.

Great golfers recognize that, because they are not machines, they will hit poor shots. They are stable and unflappable in the face of bad breaks and tough luck. They don't cave in, they bounce back.

Great golfers can be childlike in their appreciation of subtle nuances. They can savor the beauty of a golf course. Despite the threat posed by competitors, they can admire the talent of others without envy or hostility.

They are at peace with themselves and the arena in which they perform. Their mindset—as opposed to their golf swing—is something others should seek to emulate.

TIP #23:
USES OF IMAGERY

Using visualization, or imagery, is of critical importance in playing a solid round of golf. Here's a mental checklist of things to do as part of your pre-shot routine.

1. Picture the ball coming to rest at the target.
2. Picture the ball landing in the target area.
3. Picture the flight of the ball.
4. Imagine yourself executing your best swing.
5. Imagine the *feel* of that swing.
6. Tell yourself to trust your ability to execute.

TIP #24:
FORGET ABOUT YOURSELF

Regardless of physical ability, golfers can improve performance levels by learning to focus on one specific task at a time—whether it's hitting a drive, approach shot, bunker shot or putt.

Golfers must learn not to think about themselves or entertain thoughts unrelated to the task. When thoughts are internally focused, when a golfer becomes self-conscious and preoccupied with his or her own ego, anxiety tends to increase. Worry sets in. They begin to think about what doesn't feel right and what might go wrong. Negative associations multiply.

Such thoughts lead to the anticipation of negative outcomes and expected failures. And, before you know it, you've developed a mindset counterproductive to successful performance.

Control your thoughts by limiting your focus to the task at hand. Think about hitting the golf ball where you want it to go—employing visualization to cue yourself for success—and nothing else.

TIP #25:
THOUGHT REBOUNDING

The countermeasures that you use to handle those recurring pictures of failure do not include disengaging from reality. If you're on the 18th tee at Pebble Beach, with the Pacific Ocean on your left, tell yourself to hammer the ball down the right-middle of the fairway. Don't pretend the Pacific Ocean isn't there. It's like trying not to think of a white bear.

Research shows that the thoughts you're trying not to have rebound. Therefore, it's better to think about what you want to have happen—like hitting your drive in the fairway, not the ocean—and then do the work (physical and mental) you need to do to make that occur. Just as you practice to "train" your swing and make it more consistent, discipline your mind to control thoughts and emotions. Don't let negative images rebound.

TIP #26:
FOCUS ON THE
TASK AT HAND

Amateur golfers would be better served by trying to emulate the thought processes of PGA Tour players, rather than the pros' golf swings.

What do the pros think about? Only the task at hand: How the situation dictates their club selection. How the lie affects the type of shot they can play. How much the wind will affect the ball's flight. Where the ball will land. How much it will roll.

Professional golfers assimilate and analyze all the pertinent data, then rivet their attention on completing the task. Develop your own talents for living in the present moment and you'll become a better player.

Ted Williams learned tricks of concentration, which helped him focus on the task at hand: hitting the ball.

TIP #27:
AN HOUR'S WORTH OF CONCENTRATION

Each shot in golf requires approximately 40 seconds to plan and execute. Some recovery shots require more than that, while some routine shots, like tap-in putts, require less. The average comes to about 40 seconds.

Assuming your average score in golf is 90 strokes, that equates to 3,600 seconds of planning and executing (40 seconds x 90 strokes)—which just so happens to be the number of seconds in one hour. A round of golf, therefore, requires only about 60 minutes (48 minutes for par-shooters) of intense concentration.

Learn how to turn your concentration skills on—and when to turn them off. You'll have more fun playing golf, and you'll play with less strain physically and mentally. You can do so without having to relax your expectations, lower your goals or decrease your ambition.

TIP #28:
CONCENTRATION IS KEY

In his endearing and often inadvertent wisdom, Yogi Berra, the New York Yankees' Hall of Fame catcher, once said that the game of baseball was "90 percent mental, and the other half, physical."

Every golfer, including Yogi, who was one of my golf partners during his days as a coach for the Houston Astros, recognizes that golf is the most mentally challenging of all sports. Finding the right things to think about—to concentrate on—is the real key to playing high-level golf.

One of the most revealing moments in golf broadcasting history occurred at the 1986 Masters, when Jack Nicklaus, in the midst of a final-round charge that earned him his sixth Masters championship, reached the 16th tee. Commentator Tom Weiskopf (who had a number of high finishes at Augusta National, but who never won a green jacket) was asked by one of his CBS colleagues what Nicklaus was thinking about.

Weiskopf erupted, "If I knew what he was thinking about, I would have won this tournament."

TIP #29:
CHANGING SELF-TALK

To make your self-talk positive, you must first be aware of any negative internal dialogue that you are having with yourself.

You must also be aware that the tone and flow of such comments have a profound influence on your emotions and motor performance—and, ultimately, on what occurs on the golf course.

You can talk yourself into a bad round. You can also talk yourself into a round where you get the most out of your game, where you don't lose any shots because of anger or negative expectations.

The skills for being more positive in your mental approach are outlined in this book. Work on them.

Changing your self-talk will help you control your anger.

TIP #30:
NEGATIVE SELF-TALK

One of the biggest detriments to good scoring in golf is negative self-talk. How many times have we seen someone verbally chastising himself, or herself, for their poor play?

"You dummy! How could you hit the ball there?"

"What a jerk I am!"

"This is ridiculous. I'm going to quit this #@@!@# game!"

All golfers have heard such phrases countless times. Many of us have said such things to ourselves at one time or other.

What we need to do is dump the negative self-talk and replace it with positive messages. Interrupt the flow of bad thoughts and bad images, substituting good thoughts and good images. Replace the inner dialogue that says you can't do something, with a voice that says you can.

"I can do this."

"I've hit this type of shot before."

"There's nothing to stop me from pulling off this shot."

Develop an inner voice that is upbeat and success-oriented, and repeat those messages to yourself over and over. In many cases, reassuring yourself that you can do something increases the chances that you will.

TIP #31:
THOUGHT STOPPAGE

When your self-talk becomes negative, when you begin berating yourself and belittling your abilities, recognize the verbal self-abuse and employ the technique of "thought stoppage."

Once you detect a negative thought or negative self-talk, simply say "Stop!" and use another thought to derail the train of negativity. Replace destructive thoughts and negative self-talk with constructive thoughts and language.

Remember a similar shot you executed successfully. Go into your personal highlight film and pull out a positive mental cue.

Thought stoppage can work for everyone. Shift your attention to positive, productive, task-related thoughts. Have a menu of positive thoughts and successful shots to call up.

TIP #32:
THE ENEMY WITHIN US

What golfers say to themselves and what they believe about themselves has a powerful influence on performance. Often on the golf course we become our own worst enemies—not, alas, our own best friends.

If you are not already a positive, optimistic, constructive person, you can learn to become one through better understanding of your self-talk. How? By confronting the negative voices that plague so many underachievers. By disputing the negative self-talk. By fighting back against the voices of doubt and deception.

When you are faced with adversity in golf, check your self-talk. Replace negative thoughts with some constructive ones. Tell yourself: "I've got this shot. I'll just go ahead and hit it close. Nobody can keep me from doing what I know how to do."

Nathaniel Hawthorne wrote: "What other dungeon is so dark as one's own heart/What jailer is so inexorable as one's self!" Hawthorne understood that we are our own worst enemies.

TIP #33:
PUT A POSITIVE SPIN ON SELF–TALK

Positive self-talk and negative self-talk have what researchers call a reciprocal relationship. That is, when positive self-talk is high, negative self-talk is low. When negative self-talk is high, positive self-talk is low.

The goal of mental training is to lower negative self-talk (which drains a golfer's mental energy) and substitute constructive, positive thoughts for counterproductive negative ones.

It's impossible to put a positive spin on your self-talk, however, until you become aware that your self-talk is negative. Conduct a check periodically during a round to make sure your self-talk is positive.

TIP #34:
SELF-REGULATION

Most of us have been taught that if we try hard enough, we have our best chance of succeeding. This is called the "drive theory" of human performance. Increasing your arousal gives you the best chance of making the putt, right? Wrong.

Most human performance problems follow what is known as the Yerkes–Dodson rule, which states there is an inverted U-shaped relationship between arousal and performance. Simply stated, when we are overaroused we perform poorly, and when we are underaroused we also perform poorly.

The optimal performance zone is somewhere in the middle. I've found this rule to be generally applicable to most sports situations. We need to avoid "overloading" and also avoid "underloading."

TIP #35:
MONITOR AROUSAL
LEVELS

Golf requires a lower level of arousal than most sports, and the shorter the shot a golfer has to play, the lower the level necessary. When delicate, highly skilled, "overlearned" movements like chipping and putting are required, you must decrease your arousal levels and physiologic responses like the heart rate and muscle tone. Whatever else you do, don't allow yourself to get too highly aroused.

To manage your arousal level better, pay attention to your own experiences and see what works best for you. If you are a high-strung individual with high levels of competitive anxiety, try gearing yourself with slow, measured breathing and by relaxing your muscles. If you are a low-key individual who needs to become more competitive, walk faster and breathe faster to increase your heart rate, and give yourself constant pep talks to raise your level of arousal.

TIP #36:
THE ONLY THING WE HAVE
TO FEAR. . .

Probably the most irrational, but easily reversible, problem in golf is the persistence of disabling fears. Imagine the reaction you'd receive from a non-golfing friend if you confessed the fear and trembling you've experienced standing over a three-foot putt. They'd probably think you were joking—or nuts.

By seeing our true skills and recognizing more clearly the true difficulty of the challenges of the tasks, we can eliminate a lot of the fear in golf.

TIP #37:
MANAGING YOUR
MISTAKES

Success in golf correlates directly with how a player handles the mistakes that inevitably occur. Good golfers manage their mistakes by forgetting immediately a poor swing or bad strategic decision and concentrating on the next challenge.

Mediocre-to-poor golfers allow mistakes to manage them. One bad shot or a series of bad shots can sabotage their entire round. These players dwell on previous shots, not the present one.

One of the best assets any golfer can possess is the attitude that mistakes are part of the game. Each mistake, rather than being a catastrophe, is an opportunity for us to learn about ourselves and our golf games.

Mark Twain, who was notorious for his dislike of golf, said that "a man can learn to deal with any adversity—as long as it's another man's!" It wouldn't be a bad idea to pretend that another player was getting the bad breaks you are; this would help to distance yourself from the adversity and cope better.

TIP #38:
THE FORGIVERS' CREED

Be your own best friend on the golf course, not your own worst enemy. When you make a mistake—and you will—be ready with these affirmations (The Forgivers' Creed):

1. I will forgive myself for all mistakes I make.
2. I will concentrate on doing my best right now, because I cannot change what has happened in the past. All I can control is giving my best effort to strive for excellence at this moment.
3. I will look at every situation as an opportunity to take a positive step toward reaching my potential.
4. I will value each mistake as an opportunity to learn.
5. I will not envelop myself in self-loathing, nor wallow in self-pity. I will be strong—and move on.

A sense of humor, and an ability to step outside yourself, helps you deal with mistakes.

TIP #39:
BEHAVIORAL CHAINS

Bad rounds in golf often have as much to do with poor behavioral chains as with bad swings or poor shot-selection. Here, sad to say, is an all-too-frequent example of a bad chain of behavior:

"I had great expectations for the club championship.... My golf swing had definitely improved.... Got too excited, too focused on the outcome.... Hit bad tee shot on first hole, made double-bogey.... Got angry.... Wondered if I'd been working on the right stuff.... Made a couple more bogeys.... Self-doubts increased.... Started to blame my teacher.... Had he been telling me the right things?... Front nine a disaster.... Angrier and more negative.... Lost in match play (or my medal score skyrocketed).... Frustrated, embarrassed, doubting ability.... Won't go back to see my coach.... Think I'll watch golf tips on TV instead.... As for the club championship, maybe next year."

When you suffer through these disheartening experiences, use a journal to write down the behavioral chain that led to disaster. Identifying and understanding the source of your problems (negative thoughts and images, poor self-talk) will help you become a better player.

You'll be able to break a bad behavioral chain before it picks up too many links.

TIP #40:
A STARTER SET OF GOALS

Goal-setting is an important skill because it influences our motivation to succeed, the direction of our efforts and the persistence to carry out our plan until we achieve success or failure. It is also important that each golfer set his own goals, and that the goals be achievable, measurable and, if they pertain to results, that they have some time-to-completion timetable.

Here's a "starter set" of golf goals that will help you prepare for your next tournament. Work out with your coach how much time to spend on each.

Training Goals:
Swing; short game; putting; on-course practice; mental rehearsal.

Tournament Goals:
Doing what it takes to get prepared; relaxing and attuning yourself; having good self-talk; developing a strategy for playing each hole; adopting a one-shot-at-a-time mentality; managing mistakes; focusing well.

Get started with goal-setting—the proper way.

TIP #41:
FIND A GOOD COACH

For improvement in any area to occur, an individual must have the right information and a good coach. Many athletes who have good coaches, and the talent to succeed at a high level, fail miserably because they never acquire the skills to be highly coachable. One of the ways in which truly great athletes differ from ordinary ones is that they are very coachable.

To give yourself a chance to learn the motor or mental skills that are keeping you from becoming a better golfer, you have to be able to trust your coach. And trust in your coach starts with respect for yourself.

If you don't have respect for yourself, if you don't have a good internal dialogue with yourself and the necessary mental toughness to convert your practice efforts into success in competition, forget it. It's not the coach's fault you fail to improve.

Finding the right coach or teacher for yourself is important.

TIP #42:
GOOD GOALS, BAD GOALS

Goal-setting is fundamental to athletic success. Setting goals clarifies our expectations and increases our focus, motivation and self-confidence. It improves our training methods and the likelihood of achieving success.

Setting goals affects performance by directing attention, mobilizing efforts, increasing persistence and aspiration to succeed, and motivating the development of strategies to improve.

Not all golf goals are good goals, however. The worst goals a golfer can set are to "break 80" or "break 90" or "break 100."

Numeric goals are results-oriented goals. They focus exclusively on outcomes, something not within a golfer's control.

Golfers should instead set "process" goals. Examples of process goals are:

- I will be relaxed and comfortable on every shot.
- I will maintain a positive attitude throughout my round, even after bad shots and mis-hits.
- I will focus on making good swings and blocking out distractions.

Such process goals are totally within any golfer's control. They play a critical role in mastering the mental game.

TIP #43:
TAKING LESSONS

Empty your mind so that you can really listen and learn from your coach. You can't achieve the proper learning approach if your mind is racing—if you are busy calculating and analyzing the ramifications of making the changes your coach suggests.

Ask relevant questions whenever you don't understand. Give feedback to your coach about how it feels for you so that he or she can learn how to communicate better with you. Then follow the advice *exactly as it's given*. If your coach tells you to perform a drill 15 times a day, and practice it in front of a mirror 50 times a day, do just that. Don't perform the drill 2,000 times, adopting the notion that "more is better."

Your responsibilities are to give clear feedback, to have a consistent and stable attitude of mental toughness and to be competitive, so that your new swing works in competition. If you can make your new techniques work in practice, you can take them into competition. Don't add any new thoughts, don't analyze and don't try any harder just because the game is on.

By changing your approach during competition, you effectively alter the memory of what you are trying to reproduce; you have reshuffled the deck. You will have broken your contract with your coach, and your patterns of performance will be inexplicably erratic. Use a consistent approach and you will get more out of yourself and your coach.

TIP #44:
A WORD TO THE
SWING DOCTORS

One hindrance to human learning is receiving too much feedback. But it seems many golf instructors want to give their students "instant feedback," using every swing to make another point.

Human performance research suggests that teachers and coaches can promote the fastest and most durable learning for their students if they *reduce*, not increase, feedback.

A recommended strategy would be to have the teacher offer his or her critique after a "block" of 10 or 12 swings, not after each swing or putt.

Golf teachers should provide a vivid picture of the correct fundamentals of the golf swing; prescribe drills and practice routines that will be the basis for learning; together with the player, set up a practice schedule with appropriate time-to-completion goals; and convey information on better practice habits and how to carry over what you learn into competition.

If you, as an aspiring golfer, are looking to measure your teacher's approach, the preceding checklist is a good beginning.

TIP #45:
PRACTICE MAKES BETTER
(NOT PERFECT)

A young tourist stops an old man on the streets of New York City and asks for directions. "How do you get to Carnegie Hall?" asks the out-of-towner. To which the old-timer replies, "Practice, practice, practice."

Seriously, how can golfers make the most of practice time?

- Simulate game conditions as closely as possible. (For example, don't just hit balls at the range. Visualize that you are playing specific shots on specific holes at your home course.)
- Practice stress-inoculation. (Practice in rain, windy conditions or when you're not feeling at your peak.)
- Space out your practice sessions. (Hitting 50 balls in eight sessions a month is more valuable than hitting 200 balls in two practice sessions.)
- Include short-game shots in every practice session. (But only if you're interested in lowering your scores.)

Practicing under stressful conditions will make you tougher under pressure.

TIP #46:
ON THE LESSON TEE

Motor learning, required for absorbing a skill like swinging a golf club or shooting a basketball, comes in three stages.

Stage one is characterized by trying to get the fundamental picture of how a particular skill is performed. Typically, this stage is marked by gross errors, and efforts are aimed at reducing the severity of mistakes. Stage one is highly cognitive, meaning that a lot of thinking is involved.

Stage two is where we begin to associate the skill with some previous success we have had with our kinesthetic (physical) or spatial awareness of the correct move.

Stage three involves precious little mental effort. The skill simply "runs off" like a computer program—automatically— without our having to put a lot of effort into the movement.

When we are novices in a sport like golf, our brains have no obvious model. Practice forms memories that allow us to make our skills durable and permanent. Later, we are able to borrow parts of memorized "programs" that the brain may have already stored.

Practice, therefore, is necessary to develop our skills to the point where they are grooved. Mastery is obtained only after the skill is "overlearned." It is then that we can move into a high-performance mode, where we simply trigger the start of the movement and the program runs off automatically. We can then free up our attention to score.

TIP #47:
TOO MUCH FEEDBACK

One of the most destructive forces in learning golf is receiving too much feedback. Many teachers—and almost all students—are guilty of over-analysis. We tend to critique each swing, or each putt, rather than groups, or series, of swings and putts.

If you over-analyze, you wind up wanting to over-correct and over-tweak. The result is you fall short of adding permanence and automaticity to your swing.

Lighten the information load and you'll get more out of your game.

TIP #48:
ACQUISITION PHASE
VERSUS PERFORMANCE
PHASE

All golfers need to recognize the difference between the acquisition phase of learning and the performance phase of execution. Never the twain shall meet.

The practice tee is the place for learning, for acquiring new skills. It's the place to shape (or re-shape) your golf swing.

The golf course is the place for performing, or executing shots. It is definitely *not* the place to work on swing mechanics or tinker with the golf swing.

Scientific research, as well as testimony from many of the best golfers in history, suggests that it's best to have only one "swing thought" on the golf course—and that it's best not to try too hard to execute it.

Trust yourself and believe in your athletic brain's ability to repeat sound mechanics. If your mechanics aren't sound and they impede the performance phase, return to the practice tee, consult a teaching professional and concentrate once again on the acquisition phase.

Mike Schmidt, the best third baseman in baseball history, uses his knowledge of sound
mechanics to compete on the Nike and CGA
Tours.

TIP #49:
THE CONCEPT OF
OVERLEARNING

The good news about learning a complex motor skill, like the golf swing, is that once we have mastered the task—"overlearned" it, in fact—the memory of how to perform the skill is permanent. It resists decay.

An analogy would be riding a bike. As children, most of us learned how to ride bikes. It was difficult at first and required a great deal of thinking (cognitive effort) about how to do it, but once we learned how to pedal, keep our balance, use the brakes and (when necessary) fall, we were set.

We developed permanence by overlearning the skill once we had mastered the technique. Many of us who haven't ridden a bicycle in years could, if we so desired, hop on one tomorrow and pedal to our heart's content.

The same principle applies to the golf swing. It can be mastered and overlearned. One goal of every golfer should be to learn the movement, develop a strong internal representation (what's known as "muscle memory") and practice the swing until it's overlearned.

At that point, you will be able to play golf like you ride a bike—without thinking about the mechanics involved. You'll be free to turn your thoughts to the mental game.

TIP #50:
WHY PRACTICE?

The objective of practice is so that you can learn and retain both physical and mental skills over a long period of time (and perhaps even during long periods of non-use of these skills). How can we learn these methods and prevent *decay*—that is, the loss, or degrading, of these skills?

One of the factors that will determine how much you can learn and how long you can retain it is how deeply, strongly and elaborately you have processed the motor and mental information. Have you practiced well, transferred it to the course and mentally rehearsed what you have learned? Forgetting and skill degradation are caused by the decay of a memory trace. If you don't practice and develop an adequate mental representation of your swing, it will decay.

The other detriment to your learning and retention is interference. Are you entertaining other information that detracts from achieving a clear concept of your swing? Interference, off-target practice or no practice at all makes memory traces (or the internal representation of your swing) weaker and more difficult to recover, especially under pressure.

TIP #51:
PUT IT IN WRITING

Serious golfers (read: winners) will use a journal, or note-book, to keep track of what part of the game they are working on and what progress they are making. These journals serve as information logs about practice, fitness and diet, as well as family, spiritual and mental goals.

Human learning is a trial-and-error process. By keeping a journal, we can see what is working in our golf games—and what isn't.

TIP #52:
SHORT–GAME SUCCESS

If you are committed to playing better golf, and shooting lower scores, you must make short-game skills the focal point of your training and preparation.

Achieving short-game success requires developing a quiet mind. Rely on your natural athletic gifts to respond to the target. Focus your attention more on the target than on the ball. Once you have trained yourself to stick to your mechanics, your stroke will become automatic.

That frees you up to attend to the most important stimulus—the target.

Baseball Hall of Famer Johnny Bench understands the key to better golf for him is the short game.

TIP #53:
VISUALIZE SUCCESS,
NOT FAILURE

One way to play better golf is to *see* yourself executing a shot successfully before you swing the golf club. This mental rehearsal is an important part of all professional sports.

The practice swings you see professionals take as part of their pre-shot routines serve as both their physical cues and mental cues. Many pros actually see themselves pulling off a particular shot before making their play.

Jack Nicklaus, for example, has said many times that he would never take the putter back until he saw himself in his mind's eye stroking his ball along the intended path and into the cup.

Too many high-handicappers, however, employ no visualization techniques. Or, even worse, they visualize failure.

If there is water surrounding a green, it's the water they see, not the green. If there is a bunker between their ball and the green, they see themselves hitting into the sand. If they are already in a bunker, they see themselves unable to get out.

If you're looking at the trouble spots on a golf course, chances are you'll find them. Look instead to the wide fairways and open greens, and see yourself maneuvering your ball to safe areas.

Visualizing success, not failure, gives you a head start on executing a particular shot.

TIP #54:
EMERSONIAN
SELF–RELIANCE

If you study the golf swings of Ben Hogan, Sam Snead and Byron Nelson, you see dramatic differences. These three great champions, however, demonstrate the wisdom and veracity of Ralph Waldo Emerson's philosophy and psychology of self-reliance. Emerson implored each person to know himself, trust his instincts and recognize his own genius.

Hogan, Snead and Nelson were proof of the Emersonian principle that we have to believe in ourselves and believe in *our own system* in order to succeed in any endeavor. Emerson also argued that "Imitation is suicide."

He would have made a great sports psychologist.

*Ralph Waldo Emerson
implored us to trust our-
selves and not be copycats.*

TIP #55:
UNDERSTANDING
YOURSELF

All different types of personalities—gregarious, reserved, contemplative, off-the-cuff, dour, jolly, aggressive, conservative, sophisticated—can be successful in golf. For example, look at the differences among the immortal trio of Ben Hogan, Sam Snead and Byron Nelson.

Hogan was tough, introverted, cold, formal, aggressive and highly disciplined. Snead, a natural showman, was extroverted, talkative and congenial. Nelson was boot-tough in competition, but otherwise warm, sensitive and modest.

They were as different as morning, noon and night, but each possessed a fundamental understanding of himself, which helped each to maximize his unique abilities.

A critical key to performance for any golfer is to understand yourself. How you think, act and react. How you train and condition yourself to succeed. Knowing what is best for you—and thinking and acting accordingly—will allow you to give the best performance you are capable of giving.

TIP #56:
PLAYING TO WIN

Ben Hogan, Sam Snead and Byron Nelson were the towering names in American golf in the pre-Arnold Palmer era. Hogan was the consummate study in concentration, Snead was the most naturally athletic golfer, and Nelson was a model of consistency.

What did they have in common? A desire to excel.

"The thing was, each of us wanted to beat somebody," said Nelson. "And it wasn't just that we wanted to beat somebody, but we wanted to perform the best that we could perform.

"I think that was the main thing we had in common, wanting to play the best that we could play. We did not want to get beat. It wasn't that we hated anybody, or anything, but competitively, we wanted to win."

Win they did. Snead (81 tournament wins), Hogan (63 wins) and Nelson (52 wins) are three of the five winningest players in PGA Tour history. Jack Nicklaus (70 wins) and Arnold Palmer (60 wins) are positioned among the memorable trio.

TIP #57:
TEMPERING YOUR
PERFECTIONISM

We should not expect perfection in our golf games. We're human beings; we make mistakes. Even a great ball-striker like Ben Hogan has said that during an 18-hole round of golf, he only hit a few shots to his complete satisfaction.

Instead, golfers should attempt to temper perfectionism, because making mistakes is part of the game.

One of the most significant differences between professional golfers and amateurs is that the pros don't verbally abuse themselves after a bad shot. They might be miffed, but they immediately re-channel their thoughts to the next shot. They don't dwell on what has just transpired—something over which they have no control.

The lesson here is not to be too hard on yourself when something goes wrong—because it will. Rather, focus on making a better swing on the next shot.

Dan Quayle can hit the ball like a PGA pro, but by trying to be perfect he can hit mediocre shots.

TIP #58:
HOGAN'S PREPARATION

While a young reporter for the now-defunct *Fort Worth Press*, noted golf writer Dan Jenkins was assigned to write about Ben Hogan's preparation for the 1951 U.S. Open at Oakland Hills.

Jenkins recalls watching in amazement as Hogan took out a 3-iron and began hitting scores of low, left-to-right shots that traveled about 150 yards.

"What on earth are you doing?" asked the inquiring mind.

"I might need that shot at Oakland Hills," responded the ever-calculating Hogan.

All the preparation paid off. Hogan won the U.S. Open, for a third time, at Oakland Hills, his final round 67 eliciting the famous comment, "I brought this monster to its knees."

When you practice, work on the specific shots you need to play your home course, especially ones that give you particular difficulty. With this type of focused preparation, you too can bring these "monsters" to their knees.

*Ben Hogan brought the Oakland Hills "mon-
ster" to its knees.*

TIP #59:
THE REAL HOGAN SECRET

Ben Hogan's golf swing is still the most analyzed, imitated and envied in the history of the game. In the mid–1950s, *Life* magazine paid him $10,000—an exorbitant sum at that time—to reveal the secret of his swing technique.

Hogan later collaborated with celebrated golf writer Herbert Warren Wind on *Five Lessons: The Modern Fundamentals of Golf*, which ranks as one of the most influential golf treatises ever published.

Yet despite all the invaluable information Hogan imparted to golfers, despite all his expertise about the mechanics of the golf swing, Hogan's greatest asset—his real secret—was his *mind*. Hogan's mental game was second to none.

I recommend that golfers read (or re-read) *Five Lessons*, focusing less on what Hogan says about the physical aspects of the swing, and more on his comments about the mental side of golf. Those observations alone will serve as an important resource for any golfer seeking to improve.

TIP #60:
HOGAN'S FOCUS

Ben Hogan took a scientific, analytical approach to golf. His method was labor-intensive. He sought information and feedback. He moved the dirt.

Hogan was golf's ultimate grinder. He blocked out the world around him, concentrating solely on the task at hand.

Paired with Claude Harmon at The Masters, Hogan watched his fellow competitor ace the famous par–3 12th hole at Augusta National. Hogan himself birdied the hole.

As they waited on the 13th tee, Hogan remarked to Harmon, "You know, Claude, I'm not sure I've ever birdied that hole before."

Talk about single-mindedness and focus. Hogan was the master.

TIP #61:
SNEAD'S AROUSAL

Sam Snead often said that his best mental state for performance was what he called "cool mad"—a frame of mind in which he was intense and goal-oriented, but not distracted by negative thoughts or emotions.

Snead was a proponent (as are many of the world's best players) of visualization. He prepared for a tournament by visualizing how he would play each hole. Once in competition, he visualized both the swing he wanted to produce and the type of shot he wanted to hit.

Snead believed in being 100 percent committed to each shot, then using 85 percent physical effort on most shots. The formula, obviously, worked exceedingly well for the West Virginian.

Dan Quinn is an excellent golfer and an NHL star. Quinn knows that the proper state for checking a hockey player is different from driving a golf ball.

TIP #62:
SNEAD'S SOLUTION
(LESS IS MORE)

Some golfers unwittingly fall into the trap of information over-load: They become so consumed with swing mechanics, they get in their own way. "Paralysis by analysis" is the descriptive term for this all-too-familiar condition.

The legendary Sam Snead once observed that one of the biggest problems with his colleagues on the PGA Tour was the fact that many of them would get "over-pro'd."

When Snead got out of whack, which was rare, he did not immediately start tinkering with his swing. "To correct things, I try not to change a thing," he said.

Golfers who are prone to information overload might find Sam Snead's "less is more" adjustment technique extremely useful for developing a consistent swing.

TIP #63:
TRUST YOUR SWING

After Byron Nelson became a champion in the 1930s, he never again changed his golf swing. Compare that with many of today's PGA Tour players, who are constantly tweaking their swings. Swing changes have, in some cases, led golfers down the road to oblivion.

"After five years of learning how to use a steel shaft, I never changed my swing again," Nelson said. "I knew I wasn't going to play perfect all the time, but by sticking with my swing, I got away from bad rounds. I think bad rounds are basically caused because you are thinking about things that you should not be thinking about."

Nelson believes that his consistency came from his strong belief that his golf swing was "good enough."

"I was satisfied that if I kept doing what I was doing, I would miss fewer shots. That was key. Another key was that I forgot to worry because I felt I could nearly always play my miss."

TIP #64:
MAKE AN HONEST
SELF–APPRAISAL

Byron Nelson won eight PGA Tour events in 1944. His stroke average for that year was 69.67, the lowest of his career to that point.

In his off-season appraisal, however, Nelson isolated two areas in which he felt he could improve his performance: the short game and overall concentration.

"I think that it's a necessary thing to be honest with yourself," he recalled. "Don't be critical of yourself. Just be honest enough with yourself to know that you need to change something, and then work on it to change."

At the end of 1944, Nelson practiced his pitching, chipping and short-game shots. And he set one major goal for 1945: to keep his concentration and play fewer careless shots.

How did he do in 1945? Nelson lowered his stroke average more than one full shot (to 68.33) and compiled the most remarkable record in PGA Tour history—winning 18 tournaments, including an incredible 11 straight.

TIP #65:
NELSON ON MISTAKES

Even as he was winning an astounding 11 straight PGA Tour events in 1945, Byron Nelson was making his share of mistakes on the golf course. Granted, maybe not as many as his fellow competitors, but mistakes just the same.

"Sure, I missed golf shots," Nelson remembered. "Every golfer is going to miss shots. One thing that every good player must learn is that 'I've got some shots to miss.'"

Another lesson golfers must learn, Nelson added, is to not get down on themselves. "Whenever you miss a shot, you don't need to have a negative attitude about it. You don't want to think about what you've just done because you have another shot to play."

TIP #66:
NELSON'S MENTAL
REHEARSAL

Byron Nelson likes to say that the best golf lessons he gave himself came at four o'clock in the morning.

Nelson would lie quietly in bed, in the dark, and picture in his mind his golf swing and the kind of shots he wanted to play that day.

When he got to the golf course, Nelson found that those shots were easier to execute because he had been practicing them in his mind.

All golfers should employ the same method.

Byron Nelson believes the best teaching he did for himself was visualization in the early mornings.

TIP #67:
NELSON'S GOALS

What was the goal, or motivating factor, that produced the most incredible display of sustained excellence in the history of golf (by which we mean Byron Nelson's performance in 1945, when he won 11 consecutive PGA Tour events, 18 tournaments overall, and posted a stroke average of 68.33)?

It was Nelson's burning desire to buy a ranch, where he could set up a family compound with his wife and parents.

"I was playing to win, playing to win money to buy the ranch [Fairway Ranch in Roanoke, Texas, where Nelson still lives], playing to win money to buy some cattle. I think that if I had had the goal of just playing golf to win the tournament, I don't believe I could have carried that pressure. I don't think I could have carried it on that long."

Motivated by a larger goal than just shooting low numbers, Byron Nelson put together the most remarkable streak ever in golf.

Think about your own goals in golf and use that to motivate your best performance—mentally and physically.

Mario Lemieux is a great hockey player, golfer and family man because he knows what is really important and significant in his life.

TIP #68:
GO WITH THE FLOW

Byron Nelson once said that in many of his best rounds of golf, he was unaware of his score. "I played shot for shot because that was what I was thinking," he said.

"Sure, I knew that I was playing well. Sure you are conscious of what you are doing. But I think if you start saying, 'Boy, I'm five-under; I want to get to six' or 'I'm seven-under; I want to get to eight' then you put an undue amount of pressure on yourself.

"If you are feeling good that day, just let it go. Let it go, and don't try to force it. If you try to force it, then you are going to get some tension."

TIP #69:
WINNING UGLY

Walter Hagen, one of golf's greatest showmen and raconteurs, was known for "winning ugly." Hagen, a five-time winner of the PGA Championship, probably hit more pedestrian shots than any player of his stature, before or since.

Hagen, however, took all the bad shots in stride. Even after a poorly struck drive, or errant approach shot, Hagen was unflappable. He was fond of saying that three of them (mistakes) and one of them (good shots) still add up to par—4.

All golfers would benefit from adopting Hagen's mental approach. What's done is done. Rather than chastising yourself for a mistake—"You dummy, why did you hit it *there*?!?!"—you should redirect that energy into your next shot.

Make it a good one and you—like the immortal Hagen—will soon be making some memorable pars.

TIP #70:
CONCENTRATION,
NOT WORRY

Golf immortal Bobby Jones once observed that there is no more fascinating side of golf than an examination of what golfers believe to be concentration, and the methods they employ trying to concentrate. Said Jones: "When most golfers think they are concentrating, they are only worrying."

Improving concentration skills entails narrowing your focus of attention to block out distractions. And by improving your ability to concentrate, you will increase your ability to modulate relaxation and intensity levels.

Good concentration allows golfers to center their attention on the task at hand. This releases their bodies to react in an unconscious, automatic way, without the distraction of worry.

TIP #71:
FACING UP TO FEAR

Many of the mental obstacles discussed in this book are overcome by the simple recognition that *we* are creating the problems—not the golf course, not our playing partners, not our equipment. Every one of us creates an internal reality—something that feels so real we can almost touch it.

Fears are the result of mental distortions, exaggerations and irrational thinking. The greatest "winner" in golf, Jack Nicklaus, once provided some insight into his special recognition of whom the enemy really is.

Nicklaus said, "When fear starts to hit me, my best chance for overcoming it lies in facing it squarely and examining it rationally. Here's what I tell myself: 'Okay, what are you frightened of? You're obviously playing well or you wouldn't be here. Go ahead, enjoy yourself. Play one shot at a time and meet the challenge.'"

TIP #72:
CROWD? WHAT CROWD?

One of the most raucous scenes ever witnessed in tournament golf occurred during the 18-hole playoff for the 1962 U.S. Open championship at Oakmont Country Club in Pittsburgh.

The playoff involved golf's reigning superstar and matinee idol, Arnold Palmer, a 32-year-old native of Latrobe, Pennsylvania, who was pitted against a 22-year-old sensation from Columbus, Ohio, named Jack Nicklaus.

The duel between The King and The Kid got ugly—not between the participants but between the partisans. Departing from golf decorum, Arnie's Army began cheering against the burly Buckeye. "Miss it, Fat Jack," Palmer's fans heckled as Nicklaus prepared to putt.

Despite the gallery's vociferous antics, Nicklaus prevailed in the playoff, 71–74. Years later, Nicklaus was asked how the crowd at Oakmont, with its unrestrained adoration for Palmer, had affected his play.

"Crowd?" said Nicklaus. "What crowd?"

Perhaps better than any golfer in history, Jack Nicklaus has demonstrated the mental characteristic of detachment. He has the ability to operate independently of the environment, remaining apart from what is going on around him.

That mental edge is one of the reasons why Nicklaus' record of 20 wins in golf's major championships is unmatched. Or, for that matter, unapproached.

Jack Nicklaus' ability to block out distractions was a gift that enabled him to win the U.S. Open at Oakmont.

TIP #73:
WEISKOPF'S EMOTIONAL WIN

Tom Weiskopf overcame years of frustration at the 1995 U.S. Senior Open at Congressional Country Club, winning the championship by first conquering his internal demons.

The amply gifted Weiskopf admitted that insidious voices of self-doubt and disabling perfectionism had hampered his performance when he played the PGA Tour in the 1960s and 1970s.

"Championship golf is not about who hits the best shots," said Weiskopf. "It's about who does the best job of controlling his emotions."

Beyond showing maturity on the golf course and maintaining a one-shot-at-a-time attitude, Weiskopf revealed his true wisdom.

Golf is a battle of emotions. The game is about winning the battle within yourself.

TIP #74:
BE READY TO PEAK

Have you ever had one of those days, or weeks, when you just knew nothing good would happen? The more you thought about the way things were going, the less enthusiastic and more depressed you became? You may have reached the point that you convinced yourself not to enter a tournament—right? Wrong!

During the week before the 1993 U.S. Women's Open at Crooked Stick, Lauri Merten developed a serious case of the "Why even tee it up on Thursday?" blues. The day before the tournament began, however, she reconsidered whether things were as bad as she thought. She discovered that there were many reasons to feel hope, to have confidence in her ability and to have faith she could hit the shots when she came down the stretch on Sunday.

In a magnificent display of confidence under pressure, Lauri birdied two of the final three holes at Crooked Stick, while her competitors wilted under the pressure of the final round. She learned that by having hope and faith, and by adopting a positive attitude, you can pave the way to your best performance. Lauri's attitude change connected her to a flow of positive energy that produced a peak experience.

TIP #75:
HORROR MOVIES IN
THE MIND'S EYE

Visualization and mental rehearsal have many benefits. The following, however, is a dramatic illustration of how negative visualizations can affect the performance of even the greatest of golfers.

Two-time Masters champion Bernhard Langer has at times struggled with putting problems—though today he is widely acknowledged as the world's best putter. The worst of Langer's "yips" came when he was only 19 years old.

Langer provides a great lesson on the importance of visualizing what we want to happen on the putting surface, never what we *don't* want to happen. He once described his putting woes this way:

"My putting stroke was a terrible sight. The more I missed, the harder I tried, the worse I got. I expected to miss. *I visualized the ball missing.* I froze over the ball. My brain just wouldn't instruct my body how to carry out the necessary action to stroke the putt. I had no backswing at all, and the through-swing was just a blurred jab. I felt as though my hands and arms belonged to someone else."

Talk to Langer today and you know that in his putting he visualizes good things, not bad things. Do the same.

Do you suffer from horror movies in the mind's eye?

TIP #76:
DEVELOPING FAITH

Few stories in all of sports are as inspirational as Bernhard Langer's rise to the top of the world of golf. Langer's story proves that if you work hard and have an unshakable belief in yourself, you can fulfill your dreams.

Langer's life also illustrates that you don't have to be a child of privilege, that you don't have to have all the advantages that others seem to have and that it probably helps to have experienced adversity. Facing adversity forces us to use and develop all our skills.

Some events in Langer's life and career help explain why he is uncommonly focused under pressure. He turned professional at age 14 in a country (Germany) with no recognized tournament golfers and no program to develop club professionals. With the emotional support of his family, he made it on his own.

Langer has defied the odds to become one of the greatest golfers, and most mentally tough athletes, in the entire world. He has won at least one tournament for each of the past 17 years, a feat that should not be underestimated. The reason for Langer's success: faith in himself.

TIP #77:
WATSON'S CONFIDENCE

Locked in a furious duel with Jack Nicklaus at the 1982 U.S. Open at Pebble Beach, Tom Watson hit his tee shot on the par–3 17th, the penultimate hole of the championship, into the rough.

Watson surveyed the lie and immediately liked what he saw. He had a shot.

"Get it close," encouraged Bruce Edwards, Watson's caddy.

"Close?" replied Watson. "I'm going to make it."

Whereupon he did. In one of the most memorable shots in golf history, Watson pulled out his sand wedge and pitched his ball into the hole. He broke into a victory trot, pointing at Edwards with an I-told-you-so gesture.

Watson's confidence in executing one of the most crucial shots in his great career stemmed from having practiced the same type of shot at the same green before the tournament began.

Preparation, positive thinking and narrow focus of concentration combined to produce one of golf's ultimate executions.

TIP #78:
MATCH–PLAY MAGIC

Legends in golf develop because of their ability to hit great shots under pressure—Tom Watson's chip-in on the 17th hole at Pebble Beach in the 1982 U.S. Open being a prime example.

But the truth about clutch performances, especially in match play, is that seldom does a winner have to be spectacular in the stretch. Generally, the loser will find a way to lose.

A mentally tough competitor (like a Watson or a Jack Nick-laus) understands this fact. He or she often keeps steady pressure on opponents, killing them with consistency. Seldom, if ever, will you see a mentally tough player take a high-risk/high-reward option. Instead, they'll let the mentally weaker player become impatient or take unnecessary risk.

The winner generally prevails because his or her mental game is more realistic and more mature.

Rick Rhoden made a clean sweep of CGA events in 1995, a sign of toughness under pressure.

TIP #79:
CONQUERING THE YIPS

According to one study, as many as one in four golfers has experienced the most gut-wrenching of golf maladies: the yips.

The yips, which manifest themselves in the form of involuntary movements (usually on the putting green), are a brain-behavioral phenomenon. The yips have ruined the careers of many great golf champions, Ben Hogan and Tom Watson among them.

Bernhard Langer, the two-time Masters champion, is the one great contemporary player who has managed to conquer the yips. He did so by realizing that the culprit was tension, and he learned to relax his muscles while putting, so they could obey his brain.

Thanks to extraordinary mental toughness (and countless hours of practice and experimentation), Langer not only regained his putting touch, but he became better than ever with the flat blade. His peers currently consider him one of the best putters in golf.

TIP #80:
NORMAN'S MENTAL GAME

Much has been written about Greg Norman's resurgence to the top of the Sony World Rankings during 1995, about how, after working with Houston-based golf instructor Butch Harmon, Norman tightened his swing and regained his exquisite touch in the short game.

Perhaps not enough has been written about Greg Norman's mental game. He is as mentally tough as anyone competing on the PGA Tour.

Does he dwell on the negative? No.

Does he think about what might have been? No.

After what might have been a devastating loss at the 1995 U.S. Open at Shinnecock Hills, where he led through 36 holes before running out of steam on the weekend, Norman responded like the champion he is. He came back the next week and won at Hartford, surviving a Sunday shootout with old nemesis Fuzzy Zoeller.

Norman won nearly $800,000 in June 1995 alone, finishing in the top five in four consecutive events. He knew he was playing exceptionally well, so he allowed himself to ride the crest of a big wave. He didn't let the setback at Shinnecock Hills break his momentum.

One marked sign of maturity as a golfer is to put a positive spin on any results. Congratulate yourself for the good shots, and resolve to work on your weaknesses.

TIP #81:
PLAY OFFENSE

Texan Justin Leonard, one of the rising stars of the PGA Tour, enjoyed a remarkable run between 1992 and 1994, winning the U.S. Amateur Championship (1992) and the NCAA Championship (1994). These prestigious victories, as well as several other wins in major amateur events, came after Leonard changed his mental strategy and began playing more aggressively.

Leonard and his coach, Randy Smith of Royal Oaks Country Club in Dallas, reasoned that, based on improvements in his ball-striking and short-game skills, Justin was playing and putting too conservatively. Leonard made a conscious decision to "attack" more holes and play more aggressively. Lower scores soon followed.

Twice, in fact, at the 1992 U.S. Amateur at Muirfield Village, Leonard holed his approach shot from the fairway for eagle. Remarked Leonard about his new style of play, "It makes sense to shoot for the flags rather than to the middle of the greens because they put the cups where the flags are."

Justin Leonard and coach Randy Smith tune up just before winning the U.S. Amateur.

TIP #82:
A TOTAL COMMITMENT
TO IMPROVE

During semester break one year at the University of Houston, only two student-athletes were left in the dormitory—two young men who came from opposite sides of the globe and who couldn't travel home conveniently because of the cost and the importance of their work.

One was a basketball player from Nigeria named Hakeem Olajuwon. The other was a golfer from Australia named Steve Elkington. Both of them, at that tender age, had a "program" for getting to the top and staying there. Their programs seem to be working.

The winner of the 1995 PGA Championship, Elkington is a model for self-improvement in golf. He has solid fundamentals, works hard and enjoys the benefits of fruitful relationships with his family and friends. Elkington is someone who puts his whole self into his work and is never satisfied with his level of play.

Happy, yes. Satisfied, no.

TIP #83:
TRUST IS A MUST

When Greg Norman won the 1993 British Open at Royal St. George's, he capped his brilliant performance with a final round 64.

One reason for his low score was having more trust in himself. He later revealed that the one thought he had before hitting each shot was "Trust yourself. Trust your swing."

That positive thought enabled him to swing affirmatively.

TIP #84:
DON'T WORRY BETWEEN SHOTS

At the 1986 Bay Hill Classic, Joey Sindelar had played the front nine one-over when he spied a friend in his gallery.

"How are you playing?" asked the friend.

"On my way to an 80," Sindelar replied.

Between shots, Sindelar sidled over to the gallery ropes and carried on a conversation with his friend. They discussed such topics as the Boston Celtics, a favorite Italian restaurant and how the New York Mets were faring. Over the course of the next seven holes, Sindelar was seven-under-par, a stretch that included five birdies and an eagle. As he prepared to play the 17th hole, Sindelar whispered that he was having trouble with his golf swing. "Wait a minute," said his friend, in disbelief. "What game are you playing here, golf or golf swing?"

Maybe Sindelar's swing was off, but he was doing the best he could with what he had brought to the golf course that day—in part because he wasn't worrying between shots.

Joey Sindelar gives Pirozzolo a lesson on the practice tee at The Masters.

TIP #85:
THE FRED COUPLES
PARADOX

Of all the great American golfers of the current generation, probably none is more talented—or more misunderstood—than Fred Couples.

People (golf writers in particular) misinterpret his long, relaxed golf swing and easy, gentlemanly manner as evidence of a carefree, nonpurposeful attitude. In truth, Fred is just the opposite. He is a competitor of the first order.

Couples possesses a strong sense of his own identity as a golfer and gentleman. Many assume his relaxed appearance and manner must mean he doesn't care about what he's doing. Au contraire.

Couples has the capacity to dissociate himself from the two forms of anxiety—mental and physical. Like anyone else, he feels the pressure, but he is able to keep it from destroying his physical performance.

Golfers can learn many lessons from Fred Couples, not the least of which is to keep your cool in the heat of battle.

TIP #86:
BETSY KING'S TENACITY

At the LPGA Tour's Shop-Rite Classic in July 1995, Betsy King began the final round in an ignominious fashion, but in a manner familiar to high-handicap golfers. She topped her drive on the first hole, a shot she later called the worst in her 17-year career as a touring pro.

How many times have we let a poor tee shot on the first hole dictate how we feel and play that day? How often have we mentally run up a white flag, surrendering our competitive spirit and thinking, "Oh well, looks like it's going to be a long day...."

King didn't give up. She scrambled to make four on the first hole—sinking a 40-foot putt to salvage a par—and capped her round with birdies at 17 and 18 to win the tournament. The victory, the 30th in her career, earned her a spot in the LPGA's Hall of Fame.

A muffed tee shot on the first hole didn't ruin King's round. Don't let it ruin one of yours either.

TIP #87:
BE TRUE TO YOURSELF

Some golfers are feel players. Some golfers are mechanical players. You can be successful adopting either approach—as long as you are true to yourself.

Texan Ben Crenshaw, the 1995 Masters champion, is a total feel player. Fellow Texan Tom Kite, the 1992 U.S. Open champion, is a mechanical player. A testimony to the late Harvey Penick's teaching genius was that he could mold two such disparate types into great champions.

You must pay attention to your own experiences. If you play your best with a lot of "how-to" mechanical thoughts, then stick with that strategy. If you play your best with an empty mind, go with that approach.

As William Shakespeare, who for all we know was a low-handicapper, put it, "This above all, to thine own self be true."

TIP #88:
PATIENCE PAYS OFF

In the opening round of the 1985 Colonial National Invitation Tournament in Fort Worth, Joey Sindelar shot a one-over 71. He hit the ball beautifully all day, giving himself numerous chances for birdies, but the putts simply would not fall.

That evening, we discussed the importance of being patient and more accepting, staying in the present and maintaining a good target orientation. The following day, with no modifications to his golf swing, Joey shot a course record 62. Had five short putts fallen, he would have dipped into the 50s.

When a golfer trusts himself and his ability, he can be patient. By patient, we mean suppressing the tendency to want to see effects from our hard work, skill or play.

Joey had been working hard on his swing, under the tutelage of his coach and father, Joe Sindelar Sr. Good work habits combined with plenty of practice had increased Joey's confidence and trust in his golf swing.

Joey resisted the temptation to "strain for effects." He stayed within himself and, most importantly, exercised patience. He resisted the temptation to try to change anything in his mechanics or frame of mind.

The result was a course record at one of America's most respected golf clubs, the place known as "Hogan's Alley."

*Joey Sindelar knows that
hard work + discipline = success.*

TIP #89:
ROCCA'S FOCUS

Needing a birdie on the 72nd hole of the 1995 British Open at St. Andrews to tie tournament leader John Daly, Italy's Constantino Rocca watched in horror as he hit his short eagle pitch shot "fat."

Rocca recovered by taking his time to refocus on what he needed to do next: hole his third shot. Improbably, he rammed in a 70-foot birdie putt from the front of the green, tying Daly and forcing a playoff (which the American won).

Rocca's birdie, which will no doubt become part of St. Andrews lore, represented a classic example of playing one shot at a time. Faced with adversity and overwhelming odds, Rocca showed remarkable resiliency by following one of the worst shots of his career with the absolute best.

Rocca's focus teaches a good lesson to all golfers. What's done is done. Concentrate on what happens next.

TIP #90:
DEL GRECO'S IMAGES

Houston Oilers placekicker Al Del Greco is one of the best golfers among professional athletes, a fact he demonstrated by winning the NFL Cadillac Senior Golf Challenge for a third consecutive time in 1995. Del Greco frequently employs golf images to relax himself before he attempts field goals. He often tells himself, "This is just a tap-in. No problem."

Conversely, when Del Greco is on the golf course, he often uses football images to keep him focused and relaxed. A frequent image he uses on the putting green is "Hey, this is just an extra point. Hit it solid."

Anytime you feel nervous on the golf course, such as when you face a pressure shot late in a match, tell yourself to do what you know how to do. Relating to your strengths and what you have overlearned, as Del Greco does, will relax you and help you focus.

Al Del Greco "hitting it solid."

TIP #91:
LOOK FOR GOOD REASONS
WHY THINGS HAPPEN

Anders Forsbrand, a Swedish touring professional who has had good success on the European PGA Tour, set a goal of making Europe's 1995 Ryder Cup team. Despite hard work, Forsbrand failed to play up to his potential before the matches and didn't qualify for the team.

Forsbrand sought advice and inspiration from his good friend Bernhard Langer, who counseled Forsbrand on how to have a better mental approach. Meanwhile David Leadbetter, one of the world's foremost golf instructors, helped Forsbrand with his swing, by reducing his wrist-cock in the backswing.

Armed with a new attitude and better swing, Forsbrand went off to the European Open the week following the 1995 Ryder Cup matches and finished in the top 10. (His friend, Langer, won the tournament.) The following week, Forsbrand and Langer, who were staying in the same house, battled each other down the stretch at the German Masters, which Forsbrand finally won by three shots.

A miracle? Not really. The German Masters was an example of two great players peaking at the right time. For Forsbrand, the experience served as a valuable lesson: He had failed to make the Ryder Cup team because he lacked certain mental and physical skills. He worked diligently to acquire them, and he succeeded in putting them to good use.

TIP #92:
SIR CHARLES

At a celebrity golf tournament, NBA All-Star Charles Barkley drained a 30-foot birdie on the 18th green, then informed his gallery, "I've been putting like that all day."

Barkley's memory, it seems, was selective. He had neither played nor putted particularly well that day. But Sir Charles' attitude, as always, was optimistic and brimming with confidence.

When you do something special on the 18th hole, as Barkley did, give yourself permission to feel good about your game. Bring that positive attitude back to the course the next time you play.

Barkley: "I've been putting like that all day."

TIP #93:
QUAYLE KEEPS HIS HEAD

Former U.S. Vice President Dan Quayle shot one of his best rounds of golf in the 1992 AT&T Pebble Beach Pro-Am, despite the huge crowds and hoopla. Quayle was able to "soft focus" on swing mechanics and, as a result, made four birdies in the first 10 holes, including a chip-in three on the par–4 first hole.

There he blocked out "advice" from the gallery and ignored the fact he faced a difficult downhill chip from behind the green. He had one simple thought: lob the ball with a pitching wedge to an exact spot. He visualized doing so, then executed the shot perfectly. Bam—nothing but cup.

On Pebble Beach's famous finishing hole, Quayle boomed a 300-yard drive to the heart of the fairway. A costly mis-clubbing by his caddy (Dr. Fran Pirozzolo) on the second shot cost Quayle a double-bogey, however, as his ball flew the green and found the Pacific Ocean.

Overall, Quayle played an exceptional round, primarily by focusing on the task at hand. The only thing he might have done better was to account for the adrenaline rush at 18; either that or find a better caddy.

All golfers, as Quayle demonstrated that day, play their best when keeping their attention on the job to be accomplished. Limit your thoughts to the shot in front of you, not one you messed up several holes back, or a tough one you'll face later.

Quayle shows us how to focus.

TIP #94:
STICK TO YOUR PLAN

Heavyweight boxing champion Evander Holyfield lost his title to Riddick Bowe in 1992 by failing to follow his pre-fight strategy. He knew he didn't want to get into a toe-to-toe slugfest with the much-bigger Bowe, but Holyfield let that happen.

In the rematch, Holyfield regained his title belt precisely because he followed his game plan. He outboxed Bowe.

What does this have to do with golf? The point is that a golfer, like a boxer, should have a game plan.

Know exactly how you intend to play each hole at your home course. Visualize yourself making the swings and hitting the kinds of shots you wish to execute.

When you get to the golf course, stick to the intelligent game plan you have created, based on knowing what you can do.

TIP #95:
WHY HAVE A PRE–SHOT ROUTINE?

If you have observed PGA Tour or LPGA Tour players closely, you've probably noticed how carefully and painstakingly they prepare for each shot. By preparing for a golf shot the same way each time, they are leading to focused concentration and automatic performance. They are reducing tension and anxiety (which all golfers experience) by repeating something they have done thousands of times before.

Every golfer can develop and consistently use a good pre-shot routine. It becomes a security blanket to carry into the unknown world of each new shot. The pre-shot routine creates a natural, relaxed state that allows your body to perform without negative mental influence—freeing you to hit better shots.

TIP #96:
ON–COURSE PREPARATION

Develop consistent pre-shot routine mechanics, which get you in a ready state. Be conscious of the need for visualization and kinesthetic imagery. Visualize *every* shot. Recall your best swing trigger. Have simple execution swing thoughts.

Narrow your focus. Block out distractions and focus on one swing cue, knowing you have planned the right shot with the right club. Be totally committed to your approach.

Now, execute. Give 90 percent effort. Don't feel you have to put 150 percent effort into a particular shot to compensate for a lack of commitment. Playing within yourself allows you to relax and play your best. You'll almost feel as if you're holding something back.

Remember, don't think about outcomes. Just think about performing your best.

TIP #97:
A PRE–PUTT ROUTINE

Just as golfers should develop a pre-shot routine to help them execute full swings, they also need to develop a pre-putt routine. Here's how:

1. *Before* you get to the green, begin reading the terrain. Is one side of the green higher than the other? Which way does the grain of the grass run?
2. Before it's your turn to putt, take two or three practice strokes while looking at the hole. This feeds your brain a feel for the proper length and strength of your stroke.
3. When it's your turn, begin your pre-putt routine by reading the green and determining your line.
4. Step up to the ball, or just behind it, and make two practice strokes while looking at the hole.
5. Align the putter and your body to the intended line.
6. Now, block out the target and rely on the internal representation of your stroke. Do not try to control the outcome of the putt; just roll the ball on the chosen line at the right speed. Do not move your eyes.
7. After the ball has rolled a few feet, look up for feedback. Knowledge of your performance is more important than knowledge of results.

Focus on achieving your goal, which should be to read the green properly and then stroke the ball on the target line at the proper pace. The rest will take care of itself.

TIP #98:
THE POST–ROUND
ANALYSIS

Golfers must learn from their experiences—the mistakes as well as successes. While a round of golf remains fresh in your memory, rate how satisfied you were with your performance on these 10 key indicators, using the following 1-to-5 scale:

	SATISFIED			DISSATISFIED	
	1	2	3	4	5
1. Good Plan for the Round:					
2. Stayed Focused on the Shot:					
3. Battled when Things Got Tough:					
4. Stayed Positive:					
5. Good Self-Talk:					
6. Controlled Emotions:					
7. Showed Confidence:					

	SATISFIED			DISSATISFIED	
	1	2	3	4	5
8. Made the Right Adjustments:					
9. Quality of My Physical Game:					
10. Mental Toughness:					

Compile your score for the round, then compare it to subsequent rounds. Over time, the scores should become lower—a sure sign that you are becoming mentally tougher on the golf course.

TIP #99:
ADD A POST–SHOT
ROUTINE

The need to have a good pre-shot routine is stressed by nearly all professional golfers. Such a step-by-step approach to executing shots builds consistency, adjusts arousal levels, narrows focus and allows a golfer to swing freely and confidently.

There is a separate routine that's just as important: the post-shot routine. We need to think about the shots we've hit in the following manner:

Good shot? Terrific. What were the mental and physical cues that allowed me to execute the shot as planned? Right. Got 'em.

Bad shot? Hold on here. Was that a physical (grip, alignment) mistake? Did I make a mental error (wrong club)? Did I try to get too much out of the shot (self-awareness)? Okay, I see the problem. That won't happen again.

Great golfers, after hitting mediocre-to-poor shots, don't get angry or upset. They analyze the mis-hit so as to eliminate the chances of it recurring.

They use a good post-shot routine. You should, too.

TIP #100:
ART, NOT SCIENCE

Jackie Burke Jr., who won both the Masters and PGA Championship during his distinguished career, wrote in his 1954 book, *The Natural Way to Better Golf*: "We place too much emphasis on the mechanics of the golf swing, the so-called science of golf, and not enough on the art of playing golf or on our understanding of the other factors that govern human performance. What's wrong with American golf is that we are being turned into a society of shadow boxers."

That may sound like pretty severe criticism, but it's right on target. While golfers by all means should learn and practice good swing fundamentals, more importantly they should commit themselves to learning and employing the mental skills discussed in this book.

*Jackie Burke Jr. recommends that golfers not
get overwhelmed by the "science of golf."*

MENTAL GAME NOTES

FRAN PIROZZOLO is chief of the Neuropsychology Service at the Baylor College of Medicine and is a consultant to NASA. He is a member of the National Academy of Sciences Committee on Techniques to Enhance Human Performance, has written for leading sports magazines and has authored eleven books on the brain and behavior. Pirozzolo works on performance enhancement with the Houston Astros baseball team, the Houston Oilers football team and members of the U.S. Olympic teams.

RUSS PATE, a widely published freelance writer based in Dallas, is Contributing Editor for *Golf for Women*. He has written four golf books, including *Action on the First Tee* with Doug Sanders and *Greener Pastures* with Robert Landers.

The illustrations for this book are by renowned artist ERIK "OPIE" OTTERSTAD. These black-and-white pen-and-ink illustrations are a far cry from the colorful palette-knife paintings this artist is known for. However, he enjoys the challenge of different mediums. Mr. Otterstad's originals are owned by such illustrious golfers as Greg Norman, Bernard Langer, Ben Crenshaw, Jeff Maggert and former President George Bush. Mr. Otterstad currently resides in his hometown of Houston, Texas.

BARRY GOLDENBERG of Cranford, New Jersey, the official photographer of the CGA Tour, graciously contributed to this book. The CGA Tour and its commissioner, Jim Karvellas, whom we have worked with for many years, has supported this work. The CGA Tour is made up of great athletes and celebrities who play very high quality golf and contribute to numerous charitable endeavors.